GROW YOUR OWN INGREDIENTS
ICE CREAM!

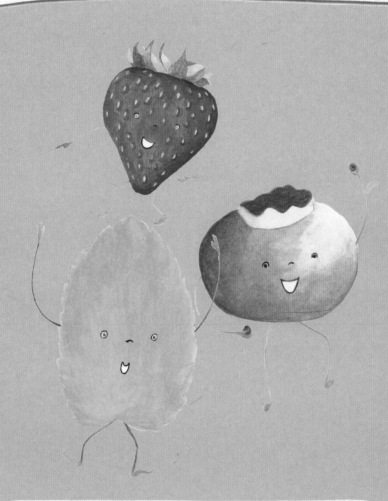

CASSIE LIVERSIDGE

Sky Pony Press
New York

I would like to dedicate this book to all the children who love to garden and cook. Keep going and spread your knowledge—you are the future!

Sky Pony Press books may be purchased in bulk at special discounts for sales promotion, corporate gifts, fund-raising, or educational purposes. Special editions can also be created to specifications. For details, contact the Special Sales Department, Sky Pony Press, 307 West 36th Street, 11th Floor, New York, NY 10018 or info@skyhorsepublishing.com.

Sky Pony® is a registered trademark of Skyhorse Publishing, Inc.®, a Delaware corporation.

Visit our website at www.skyponypress.com.

10 9 8 7 6 5 4 3 2 1

Manufactured in China, November 2014
This product conforms to CPSIA 2008

Library of Congress Cataloging-in-Publication Data is available on file.

Cover design by Cassie Liversidge and Danielle Ceccolini
Cover illustration credit Cassie Liversidge

Print ISBN: 978-1-63220-405-9
Ebook ISBN: 978-1-63220-825-5

FSC
www.fsc.org

MIX
Paper from
responsible sources
FSC® C012521

CONTENTS

Introduction

Welcome! This is my second book to help you to grow your own ingredients. In this book you will learn how to grow mint, strawberries, and blueberries, and then learn how to transform them into delicious ice cream or frozen yogurt.

TOP TIPS FOR GROWING SUCCESS!

All of these plants can be grown in pots so they are suitable for even the smallest garden space. Make sure you use a pot with good drainage holes and aim to keep the soil moist at all times. If possible, always try to use peat-free compost. Peat is a natural organic material made within the earth. It has taken thousands of years to be created and there is a limited supply.

The planting and harvesting times, given in the table below, are a general guide, as the time will depend on the variety of plant you are growing.

When best to grow:

When to plant/sow	(light)
When to harvest	(dark)

	Jan	Feb	March	April	May	June	July	Aug	Sep	Oct	Nov	Dec
Strawberry (small plants—not seeds)			plant	plant	plant	harvest	harvest	plant	plant	plant		
Mint (seeds and cutting)	plant	plant	plant	plant	plant	harvest	harvest	harvest	harvest	harvest		
Blueberry (plants)	plant	plant	plant	plant	plant	harvest	harvest	harvest	harvest	plant	plant	plant

Strawberries

It is ideal to buy small strawberry starters or plug plants in late August and September so that you can grow them before harvesting the following summer. You can also plant them during the other warmer months, too. Check the label on your strawberry plants to see if they will need any protection from frost during the winter.

Mint

You can sow mint seeds or take cuttings when the weather is warming up, from March on. The warmer summer months and longer amounts of daylight make the plants grow much quicker and stronger. Mint will die back in the winter months.

Blueberries

It is best to plant blueberry plants in the late fall so that they can grow big and strong before producing berries in the summer. Choose a variety suitable to your location and, if possible, buy more than one variety to help them produce more berries by cross-pollination.

TOP TIPS FOR ICE CREAM SUCCESS!

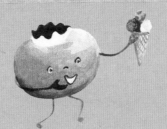

There are two ice cream recipes and one frozen yogurt recipe in this book. The mint ice cream and the blueberry frozen yogurt can be made with or without an ice cream maker. The strawberry ice cream is a no churn recipe so it doesn't require an ice cream maker. I recommend using heavy or double cream in the recipes, but you can also use whipping cream. All of the recipes are suitable for each of the flavors (i.e., you can make strawberry frozen yogurt using the fruit base with the yogurt base mixture) so you can swap the recipe to suit your taste and requirements.

You can use a recycled container to freeze your ice cream in, as long as it has a well fitting lid and shows the freezer symbol (which means it is suitable to be frozen). It is ideal to use a wide and shallow container as this makes it easiest for mixing and helps the mixture freeze quickly. Also try to put the ice cream mixture in the coldest part of your freezer (which is often at the top) so that it freezes your ice cream really quickly and improves the texture. Remember to get your ice cream or frozen yogurt out of the freezer about 10–15 minutes before you want to eat it to make it more scoop-able.

GROW YOUR OWN ICE CREAM
STRAWBERRIES

You will need . . .

Three small strawberry plants (which are called starters or seedlings). You can grow strawberries from seeds but they may take a long time to make fruit.

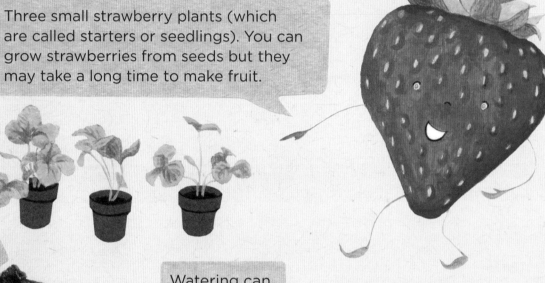

Potting compost

Watering can

A big pot or hanging basket

Straw—two handfuls

Label and a permanent marker

Top Tip: The best time to begin growing strawberry plants is in late summer or fall to give them lots of time to grow before the following summer!

STEP 1

Fill the big pot with compost almost to the top!

Potting compost

STEP 2

Make a hole with your hand in the soil.

Take the strawberry plant out of the pot and place it in the hole. Gently firm the soil around the plant.

Do the same with the other seedlings.

STRAWBERRIES

Write a label and put it in the pot.

STEP 3

Put the straw around the base of the strawberry plants. This helps keep the soil warm and moist and protects the fruit from getting eaten by snails. This is called mulch. Add more mulch in the spring each year.

STEP 4

Put the strawberry plants in a warm and sheltered place outside. Water every few days to keep the soil moist. During the winter, when there is more rainfall, they may not need much watering at all.

Top Tip: Feed your strawberries with organic plant food or use diluted "worm tea" fertilizer (plant food) made by the worms, if you have a wormery.

STEP 5

Keep looking after your strawberries through the winter by removing any dead leaves and weeds.

When it is spring again, small white flowers will grow, which turn into strawberries in the summer.

Pollen

Stamen

Carpel

Ovule

We need bees to help pollinate the flowers. This is when pollen, made by the male part of the flower (called the stamen), is moved to the female part of the flower (called the carpel). From the carpel, the pollen travels to the ovule to make seeds and fruit. Amazing!

STEP 6

Harvest your strawberries when they are lovely and red and perfect to make into ice cream! Yum!

Joke: What did one strawberry say to the other strawberry? Look at the jam you've gotten us into!

MAKE YOUR OWN STRAWBERRY ICE CREAM

To make ice cream for four people you will need:

Freshly picked strawberries
14 oz (400 g)

Condensed milk
7 oz (200 g)

CREAM

Hand whisk

Heavy (or double) cream
8 fl oz (230 ml)

Sieve

Potato masher

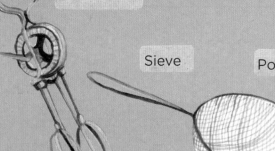

1 large mixing bowl and 1 medium sized bowl

Chopping board and knife

Storage container with a lid

You will also need scales to measure out your ingredients and space in your freezer. This is a no-churn ice cream, so you will not need an ice cream maker.

Wash your hands and put on an apron. Ask an adult for help and always be very careful in the kitchen.

Measure out all of your ingredients.

Put the strawberries into a sieve and wash under cold water.

Slice off the stems (hulls) with a knife, trying not to take off too much delicious strawberry. Then chop the strawberries into little pieces.

Put the strawberries into the medium sized bowl and mash them with a potato masher until completely squashed. Top Tip: Put a damp cloth under the bowl to keep it secure.

Put the cream into the large bowl and whisk with a hand mixer until it is thicker (be careful not to over whisk or it will become really hard).

Add the condensed milk to the cream and whisk again.

Add the fruit mixture to the creamy mixture and whisk again. This can be a bit messy but fun.

Pour the strawberry ice cream into a container and place into the freezer for at least 2–3 hours.

Remove the strawberry ice cream from the freezer about 10 minutes before you want to eat it to allow it to soften a little.

Scoop out the ice cream into cones or into a bowl and serve with fresh strawberries. So delicious!

GROW YOUR OWN ICE CREAM
MINT

You will need . . .

Mint seeds

or a cutting from a mint plant

MINT SEED

Potting compost

A watering can

A pot or recycled container with drainage holes in the bottom

Spray bottle (water sprayer)

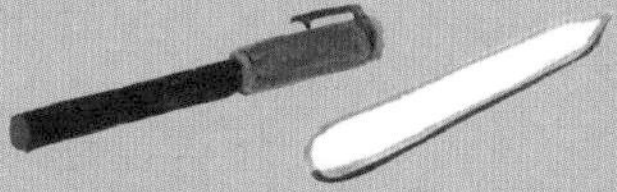

Label and permanent marker

A plastic bag and rubber band

STEP 1

Fill the pot with potting soil.

Sprinkle the seeds thinly over the soil and then cover with a small layer of potting soil. Label your plant.

MINT SEED

MINT

Spray with a water sprayer until the soil is moist.

If you have a cutting (which should measure no longer than 4 in or 10 cm), remove the bottom leaves. Place in a jar of water and leave on a sunny windowsill.

STEP 2

Seeds like a constant, warm, moist environment to germinate. Place a plastic bag over the pot and secure with a rubber band.

Keep somewhere warm and sunny like a windowsill. Remove the bag to spray the seeds with water to keep the soil moist at all times.

STEP 3

When the small seedlings have grown, remove the bag. Keep watering so the soil does not dry out.

If growing a cutting, it should have small white roots growing from the base by now.

Plant the cutting in a pot filled with potting soil and firm down. Then water it and keep the soil moist.

STEP 4

Your seedling or cutting will be strong enough to be put outside now, if the weather is warm.

Top Tip: If the pot gets very crowded, replant into a larger pot to give the plant more space to grow.

STEP 5

When your mint plants have grown lots of leaves, they are ready to be harvested to make into ice cream!

Joke: Knock knock?
Who's there?
Mint
Mint who?
Mint to tell you earlier.

MAKE YOUR OWN
MINT ICE CREAM

To make ice cream for four people you will need:

Four or five sprigs of home-grown mint (about 25 leaves)

Whole milk
9 fl oz (250 ml)

Sugar
1/2 cup (113 g)

Heavy (or double) cream
10 fl oz (300 ml)

A saucepan

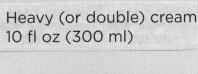

A hand whisk

A bowl

sieve

A storage container with a lid

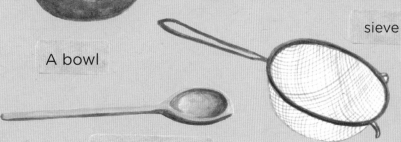

A wooden spoon

You will also need space in your freezer or an ice cream maker.

23

Wash your hands and put on an apron. Ask an adult for help and always be very careful in the kitchen.

Measure out all of your ingredients so you are ready to start.

Peel the leaves off the mint stalks. Then tear the leaves into little pieces.

Put the sugar, milk, and the torn mint leaves into a saucepan.

Ask an adult to place the pan on the burner (which is the top of the stove or cooker) on medium heat. Stir the mixture.

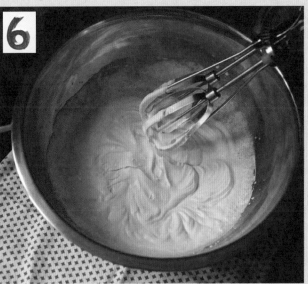

After 2–3 minutes, the mixture should be near to boiling point (when it is really bubbling). Ask an adult to remove the pan from the heat and leave it to cool.

Put the cream into a bowl and whisk with a hand mixer until it can just hold its shape and is not runny.
Top Tip: To help keep the bowl steady, put a damp cloth under it.

Strain the cooled mint mixture into the bowl of cream using a sieve.

Whisk the mixture together so that there are no lumps.

Pour the ice cream mixture into a shallow container, cover with a lid, and continue with these instructions. OR pour into an ice cream maker and follow its own instructions.

Place in a flat position in the freezer and wait for 1 hour.

Take the mixture out of the freezer after 1 hour and mix it up with a fork or spoon. The outside will freeze quicker than the inside of the mixture. Put it back into the freezer for another 1–2 hours.

It is worth the wait! Remove the mint ice cream from the freezer about 10 minutes before you want to eat it to allow it to soften a little.

Scoop out the ice cream and share with your family and friends. Delicious and minty!

GROW YOUR OWN ICE CREAM
BLUEBERRIES

You will need . . .

A two- or three-year-old blueberry plant

Acidic compost (ericaceous soil)

A watering can

Fine netting

Bark mulch (chopped-up bark)

A big pot with good drainage holes

Four canes

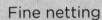

String

STEP 1

Fill the large pot with acidic compost.

Make a hole in the soil and plant the blueberry in, firming the soil around the plant.

Top Tip: Blueberry plants need acidic soil so that they can take up nutrients from the soil. Soil acidity is measured in pH. Acidic soil has a pH below 7. When the pH is above 7 it is known as alkaline and pH7 is neutral. Special acidic soil is created for blueberries and other acid-loving plants.

STEP 2

Put a layer of bark mulch around your plant to help keep the soil moist.

Place your blueberry outside in a sunny or mostly sunny place. Water it with saved rainwater if possible as it is more acidic than tap water, and it's free!

Top Tip: The leaves turn a beautiful red in the fall.

STEP 3

When bees have pollinated the blueberry flowers, fruits will form. When these fruits start to turn blue, cover the plant with a net to stop the birds from eating them.

Top Tip: The mixing of pollen by the bees from one variety of blueberry to another means you will get more berries. This is called cross-pollination. Grow more than one variety of blueberry plant if you have space.

STEP 4

Pick the berries when they are a deep blue color and use them to make into the best blueberry ice cream.

Joke: What is a ghost's favorite dessert? Boo-berry pie and I scream!

MAKE YOUR OWN BLUEBERRY FROZEN YOGURT

To make frozen yogurt for four people you will need:

Plain whole milk yogurt
18 oz (500 g)

Blueberries
10 oz (280 g)

Sugar
3/4 cup
(170 g)

Bowl

Saucepan and lid

A wooden and a metal spoon

Hand whisk

Sieve

Storage container with a lid

You will also need scales for weighing your ingredients on and space in your freezer or an ice cream maker.

Wash your hands and put on an apron. Ask an adult for help, and always be very careful in the kitchen.

Measure out all of your ingredients so you are ready to start.

Put the berries into a sieve and wash with cold water.

Put the berries into a saucepan. Add the sugar, and cover with a lid.

Ask an adult to place the pan on the burner (which is the top of the stove or cooker) on low heat. Stir the mixture every few minutes, replacing the lid.

Remove the lid after 2–3 minutes and turn the heat up to medium.

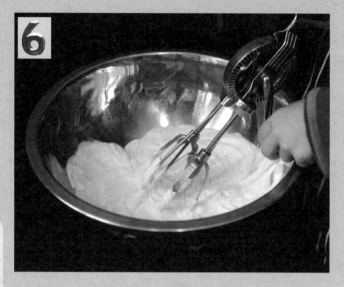

After 6–8 minutes the sugar will have dissolved and the berries will have broken down to form a blueberry mush. Remove from the heat and cool for 4–5 minutes.

Pour the yogurt into a bowl and whisk for 5 minutes.

Place a sieve on top of the yogurt bowl and pour the blueberry mixture in. Squash the mixture through the sieve using a metal spoon, until all the juice is removed. Whisk again until mixed

Pour the mixture into an ice cream maker and follow its instructions. OR pour into a shallow container and cover with a lid and keep following these instructions.

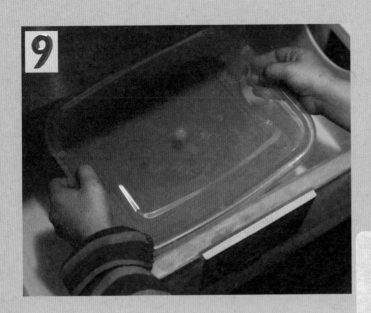

Place the container in a flat position in the freezer and wait for 1 hour.

Take the mixture out of the freezer after 1 hour and mix it up with a fork or spoon. The outside will freeze quicker than the inside of the mixture. Put it back into the freezer for another 2–3 hours.

Remove the frozen yogurt from the freezer about 10 minutes before you want to eat it to allow it to soften a little. Serve in a cone or in a bowl. Yum!

A BIT OF SCIENCE!

How to Make Ice Cream in a Bag!

You will need:
7 fl oz (200 ml) heavy or double cream
3 tbsp (80 g) sugar
7 oz (200 g) crushed strawberries or blueberries
40 oz or 2 ½ lbs (1 kg) ice cubes
15 oz or 1 lb (425 g) rock salt
1 sieve or colander
1 bowl (with pouring lip if possible)
2 jugs
Potato masher
2 medium zipper storage bags
1 extra large zipper storage bag
Thick tea towel or oven mitts

Wash your hands and put on an apron. Get all the equipment ready and weigh out your ingredients.

Wash the fruit in a colander under cold water. Cut the stalks off of the strawberries and chop into little pieces. Place in a bowl and add the sugar.

Using the potato masher, mash the fruit until it is really squashed.

Pour your cream into a jug and then add the fruit mixture.

Put the medium zipper bag into the other jug so that it is supported, folding the top of the bag around the edge of the jug. Pour in the ice cream mixture and seal the bag completely.

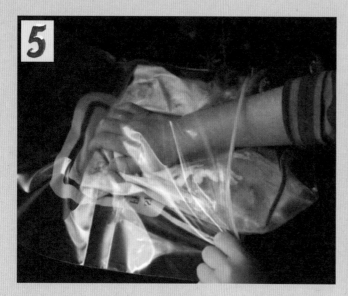

Put this bag into another medium sized bag to make sure no mixture escapes.

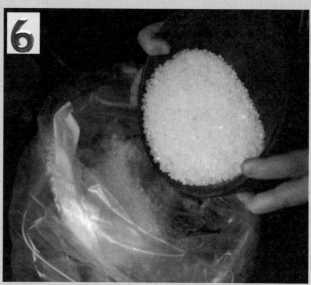

Then put the ice and salt into the large zipper bag.

Place the ice cream mixture into the ice bag so it is surrounded by ice. Then zip up the outer ice bag.

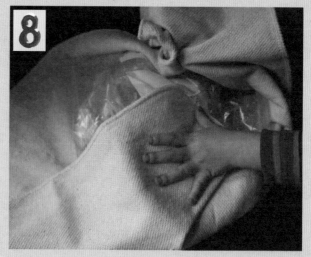

Wrap the bags in a tea towel or hold it using oven mitts. Shake the bag, agitating the ice around the mixture.

After at least 10 minutes of shaking you should be able to feel that the liquid ice cream mixture has turned into a more solid, frozen mixture. Lift out the ice cream mixture bag from the ice bag and spoon into a bowl. Enjoy making ice cream without a freezer!

How does this work? Freezing is the process of a liquid turning into a solid. Water freezes at 32°F (0°C). Melting is the process of a solid turning into a liquid.

Your ice cubes will start to melt and turn into water when taken out of the freezer because of the warmer air temperature. When you put salt into the ice cube bag, the salt molecules dissolve and mix with the water molecules. Salty water freezes at a lower temperature than just water, around -5.8°F (-21°C) depending on the quantity of salt. The temperature within the salty water ice bag drops, so when you put this next to your ice cream mixture, it lowers its temperature also. The ice cream mixture gets colder and starts to freeze.

ACKNOWLEDGMENTS

I would like to thank the following for all their help and support in the production of this book: Julie Matysik and all at Sky Pony Press for their continued support; my brilliant agent Isabel Atherton (Creative Authors); Peter Liversidge for the photography; George and Thomas Liversidge for tasting so much ice cream; Levin Haegele, Peter Foolen, Jill Feuerstein, Sally Orrock, Sammy Squire, the Willis family, Rubina Aga, Giuseppe Pollifrone; and all the wonderful children, parents, and teachers who help at my Edible School Playgrounds in London.

For more information about growing your own ingredients, please see my website: www.cassieliversidge.com.

You can also follow me on Facebook at https://www.facebook.com/GrowYourOwnIngredients or on Twitter @Cass_Liversidge.

Other books by the author:
Pasta Sauce!: Grow Your Own Ingredients
Homegrown Tea: An Illustrated Guide to Planting, Harvesting, and Blending Teas and Tisanes